# Jesus Our Savior

## The Story God's Son for Children

Adapted by Patricia Szczebak

Illustrated by Mary Joseph Peterson, FSP

Pauline
BOOKS & MEDIA
Boston

*Nihil Obstat:*
Reverend Thomas W. Buckley, S.T.D., S.S.L.

*Imprimatur:*
✠ Seán Cardinal O'Malley, O.F.M. Cap.
Archbishop of Boston

Library of Congress Control Number: 2017959726

CIP data is available.

ISBN 10: 0-8198-4023-8
ISBN 13: 978-0-8198-4023-3

Adapted from *My First Book about Jesus* written by Mary Elizabeth Tebo, FSP
© 2008, Daughters of St. Paul

Adapted by Patricia Szczebak

Cover design and illustrations by Mary Joseph Peterson, FSP



Published by Pauline Books & Media, 50 Saint Pauls Avenue, Boston, MA 02130–3491

Printed in the U.S.A.

JOS VSAUSAPEOILL11-2110105 4023-8

www.pauline.org

Pauline Books & Media is the publishing house of the Daughters of St. Paul, an international congregation of women religious serving the Church with the communications media.

1 2 3 4 5 6 7 8 9 22 21 20 19 18

# Contents

# Introduction

Did you know that the Bible is really a collection of many books? Long ago, God inspired writers to record the story of God's love for all people. Each of these inspired writings forms a book in the Bible, or Scripture. Pick up any Bible and you will find many different types of writing. Scripture includes myths, history, poems, laws, songs, letters, visions, dreams, and even building instructions!

The Bible has two parts. The Old Testament tells the story of God's Chosen People learning about God's love and waiting for the birth of the Savior. The New Testament tells the story of the life of Jesus and the early Church. We can read about many things that Jesus said and did in the books of the New Testament that we call the Gospels. There are four Gospels: Matthew, Mark, Luke, and John.

The story of Jesus really begins at the beginning of the Bible. In the first book of the Old Testament, we learn God's plan for us to live in friendship with him and enjoy the beautiful world he created. But when the first man and woman disobeyed God, they broke this friendship. Their actions brought sin and death into the world.

Because he loves us, God promised that one day he would send us a Savior who would repair that friendship. After many, many years, God the Father sent his Son to Earth. His name is Jesus, and he came to free us from our sinfulness. This is his story.

# Mother of God

A long time ago there was a young Jewish woman named Mary. She lived in the land of Israel in the city of Nazareth. Mary loved God very much. She was very happy and was engaged to a good man named Joseph.

One day, God sent the Archangel Gabriel to her. "Hail Mary," Gabriel greeted her. "God has chosen you to be the mother of his Son."

"How can this happen?" Mary asked in surprise. "I am not married yet."

"The Holy Spirit will come to you," Gabriel explained. "Your child will be the Messiah—the Savior God has promised to Israel."

Mary wanted to do whatever God wanted. She closed her eyes and said, "May God's will be done in me." At that

moment, the Holy Spirit came upon Mary, and Jesus began to grow within her as all babies grow within their mothers.

"Mary," the angel continued. "Nothing is impossible for the Lord. Your cousin Elizabeth, who is very old, is going to have a baby, too."

After Gabriel left, Mary traveled to visit her cousin. She wanted to help Elizabeth in any way she could.

When Elizabeth saw her cousin, she went out to greet Mary.

"Blessed are you, Mary," Elizabeth said. "And blessed is the baby in your womb!"

Elizabeth was so happy that Mary and the unborn Jesus were visiting her—even Elizabeth's unborn baby was joyful. He leaped in Elizabeth's womb when he heard Mary speak! Mary stayed with her cousin for three months. Elizabeth gave birth to a baby boy and named him John. Then Mary returned to Nazareth.

When Mary arrived home, Joseph was very glad. His bride-to-be was back! Then he saw that she was pregnant. *What shall I do?* he wondered. *I am not the baby's father. How can I marry her?*

That night God sent an angel to appear to Joseph in a dream.

"Do not be afraid," the angel said. "Mary's baby is from God the Holy Spirit. Make Mary your wife and name the child Jesus." Joseph trusted God and did what the angel commanded.

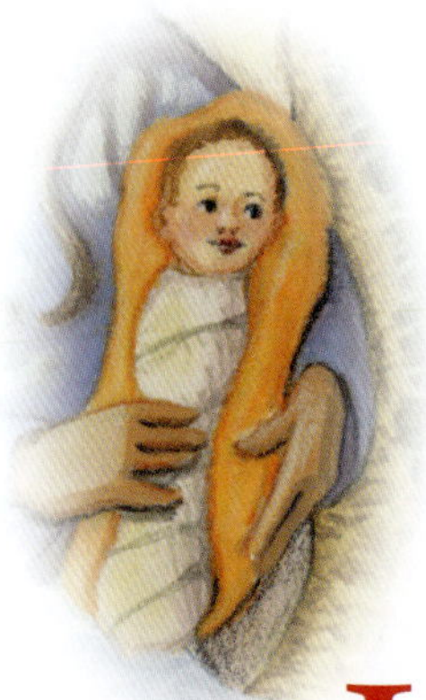

# Jesus Is Born

Some months after Joseph and Mary became husband and wife, the Roman emperor announced that he wanted all the people in the empire counted. He ordered everyone to return to their hometowns for the census. Mary and Joseph had to leave immediately for the city of Bethlehem. Mary rode on a little donkey. It was a long and difficult trip.

When they reached Bethlehem, Mary said, "Joseph, I think the baby will be born tonight. We need to find a place to stay."

Joseph was very worried. There were so many people there for the census. They could not find a place to stay.

Finally, Joseph knocked on the door of an inn, and the innkeeper answered.

"You must be looking for shelter," said the friendly man. "There are no rooms here. There are no rooms available anywhere. But, you can stay in a cave not far from here. I use it as a stable for animals. It's not very nice, but at least it's warm and dry."

Mary and Joseph followed the kind man to the cave. That very night, Jesus was born! Mary wrapped her son in soft cloths. Then she laid him in the manger filled with hay.

That night, on nearby hills, there were some shepherds. They were taking care of their sheep. Suddenly an angel appeared to the shepherds. They were terrified.

The angel said, "Don't be afraid! I have good news for you and for all people. The Savior has been born today. It is the Lord! You will find him in a cave lying in a manger."

Then many angels filled the sky. They sang, "Glory to God in the highest, and peace to his people on earth."

The shepherds went at once to Bethlehem. They found Jesus lying in the manger, just as the angel had said.

"Praise God!" said one of the shepherds as he knelt before Jesus. Filled with awe, the shepherds bowed their heads.

Later three wise men from the East arrived. They had followed a bright star that had suddenly appeared in the sky. They believed that this was a sign that a new king had been born. The wise men went to Jerusalem first. After speaking with King Herod, they followed the star to the place where Mary, Joseph, and Jesus were.

The first wise man said to Mary and Joseph, "We have come to worship the Savior." He knelt before the sleeping baby. Then he put a gift in the hay. He said, "I offer precious gold to the newborn King."

The second wise man came forward. "I give the gift of frankincense for the King who is also God."

The third wise man knelt and said, "I bring myrrh to the newborn King who will suffer to save his people."

Mary looked at her sleeping baby with love and marveled at all God had done.

# The Promised Messiah

Forty days after Jesus' birth Joseph and Mary took him to the Temple in Jerusalem. They went to present Jesus to God. This is what all Jewish families did with their firstborn sons.

There was a holy man named Simeon in Jerusalem. God had let him know that he would someday meet the Messiah. The day that Mary and Joseph came to the Temple, Simeon was there praying. He was very happy when he saw Jesus in Mary's arms. Simeon prayed, "O God, now I have seen your salvation. This child will be a light to all people."

There was also a holy woman in the Temple. Her name was Anna. She praised God when she saw Jesus. Anna told everyone that he was the child that faithful Jewish people had been waiting for.

Joseph and Mary were amazed at everything they heard. Mary looked at the sleeping baby in her arms.

"Jesus is the Savior," she whispered to Joseph. "He is the answer to God's promise of long ago." They wondered what little Jesus would say and do as he grew up. But right then, he was theirs to care for and protect.

One night an angel warned Joseph in a dream. The angel told him that Bethlehem was no longer safe for Jesus. King Herod had heard that the new King of the Jews had been born. Herod did not want the baby to take his place. The king sent his soldiers to kill all boys in Bethlehem that were younger than two years old.

"You must escape this very night!" the angel said.

Joseph woke Mary. They quickly prepared to leave. While it was still night, Joseph took Mary and Jesus to another country. The family lived in Egypt until it was safe to return to Israel.

The family settled in Nazareth. There young Jesus learned carpentry from Joseph and helped his mother with household tasks. The family was devout, and Jesus learned how to live the Jewish faith from both Mary and Joseph. He read the Scriptures and learned to follow the Ten Commandments. They were a happy and holy family.

# My Father's House

Every year faithful Jewish families went to Jerusalem to celebrate Passover. Joseph, Mary, and Jesus always traveled with a large group of friends. When Jesus was twelve years old, the Holy Family made their usual trip. After the celebration, the family began the return journey to Nazareth. Mary thought Jesus was with Joseph. Joseph thought that Jesus was with his mother. Soon Mary and Joseph discovered that Jesus was missing. They searched for him among their friends.

*What happened to my son?* Mary wondered.

Mary and Joseph looked for Jesus all over Jerusalem. They searched for three days, but they did not find him. Then Mary and Joseph decided to go to the Temple.

There they found Jesus talking with the teachers. The wise Jewish leaders were asking Jesus questions and

listening to his answers. His understanding amazed them.

Mary ran up to Jesus and hugged him. “We’ve looked everywhere for you! Why have you done this?”

“Why did you search for me?” Jesus asked. “Didn’t you know I would be in my Father’s house?”

Jesus’ answer puzzled Mary and Joseph, but they were relieved to have found him safe and sound.

Jesus went home with Mary and Joseph and obeyed them. In Nazareth, he grew in wisdom and grace. He stayed there until he was an adult and it was time to begin his work as the Son of God.

# This Is My Son

Just as Jesus grew up, so did John, Elizabeth's son. John preached to crowds of people. He told them, "You must be sorry for your sins and turn back to God." John baptized those people who wanted to be forgiven for their sins. That is why he is known as John the Baptist.

"Show that you are sorry by doing good for others," John the Baptist told the people gathered by the Jordan River. "Someone who has two coats should give one to another who has nothing to keep him warm. Whoever has extra food should give it to someone who has none."

Some people asked John if he was the Messiah.

"No," John replied. "I only baptize with water. Someone is coming who will baptize people with fire and the Holy Spirit."

One day John looked up from the river and saw Jesus walking toward him.

"I want you to baptize me," said Jesus.

John knew Jesus was the Messiah. John shook his head and said, "I should be baptized by *you*."

Jesus replied, "We must do what God wants." Jesus then stepped into the river and John baptized him.

As John poured water over Jesus, they heard a voice from heaven: "This is my Son, whom I love very much."

Then John saw the Holy Spirit—in the form of a snow-white dove—come to Jesus. John was amazed. As he preached and baptized other people, he told them about Jesus.

The Holy Spirit led Jesus to the desert after his baptism. He was there for forty days. During that time he fasted from food. Satan then tempted Jesus three times. He promised Jesus food, great wealth, and power.

Jesus responded, "Scripture says to worship only the Lord. I will obey my Father in heaven." Satan left Jesus, and angels appeared to take care of him. Then, filled with the Holy Spirit, Jesus left the desert and returned to Galilee.

# Follow Me

One morning Jesus was walking along the Sea of Galilee. From the shore he saw Peter and his brother Andrew. He also saw James and his brother John. They were in their fishing boats. Jesus told them to sail into deep water and toss their nets.

Peter said, “Master, we haven’t caught anything even though we fished all night. But at your word, we will try again.”

The fishermen lowered their nets. Before long they felt tugging in their hands. It took all their strength to pull the filled nets into the boats. The four men caught so many fish that their boats almost sank! Peter and the others were astonished.

When the fishermen reached the shore Jesus said, "Follow me. From now on you will fish for people!"

They immediately left their boats and their families to follow Jesus.

Another time, Jesus met a tax collector named Matthew. Most tax collectors were disliked because they were dishonest and kept for themselves some of the money they collected. That evening, Jesus ate dinner with Matthew and others.

"Why does Jesus eat with sinners?" one religious leader asked. "Why is he friendly with someone who steals from others?"

Jesus answered, "Only the sick need a doctor. I have come to bring mercy to sinners who are sorry for their sins."

From that day forward, Matthew became one of Jesus' followers. Many other people became Jesus' disciples. They learned from Jesus how God wanted them to live and how much God loves them.

One night, Jesus prayed to God the Father. The next morning, Jesus chose from his disciples twelve men to be his special followers—his Apostles. They would pass on to others what they learned from Jesus. Their names were Peter, Andrew, James, John, Philip, Bartholomew, Matthew, Thomas, another man called James, Simon, Judas—the son of James, and Judas Iscariot.

# The First Miracle

Jesus, some of his disciples, and his mother were invited to a wedding in Cana. During the feast, Mary noticed that the wine was running out. If that happened, the celebration would be ruined and the couple would be very embarrassed.

Mary whispered to her son, “They have no more wine.”

“What can I do?” Jesus asked. “It’s not my time yet.”

But Mary knew he would help. She told the servants, “Do whatever he tells you.”

Jesus asked them to fill stone jars with water. Each jar held twenty gallons. When they finished, Jesus told the servants to take some out and give it to the head steward.

The steward tasted what the servants had given him. He said to the groom, “This is the best wine I’ve ever had!”

The servants who had drawn the water couldn't believe Jesus had turned it into wine.

This was the first of Jesus' many miracles.

# Jesus Teaches

Jesus traveled all over Israel. He taught people about the kingdom of God. Often he told stories to help people understand what he meant. In one story, Jesus told the crowd that the kingdom of God is like the most amazing buried treasure we could ever discover.

Jesus also taught his disciples about God's merciful love. He told this story:

"There was a son who said, 'Father, give me my share of the family money. I want to leave and make a good life for myself.' But once he had the money, the son moved away and wasted all of it in sinful behavior. He ended up poor, alone, and hungry.

"The young man then decided to go back home. *Maybe my father will hire me*, he thought. *Even my father's servants eat better than I do now.*

"When he arrived home, his father came running to meet him. The son said, 'Father, I am so sorry. I have sinned against you and against God!'

"But his father welcomed him home with open arms and a loving heart. He cried out with joy, 'My son was lost, and now he has been found!'"

Jesus told this story to help the Apostles understand that God the Father forgives people who are sorry for their sins.

One day, Jesus taught his disciples a lesson about the kingdom of God by welcoming children. Many people around Jesus were bringing their children close so that they could touch him. The disciples tried to move the children away from Jesus.

"Don't stop them," said Jesus. "Let the children come to me. The kingdom of heaven belongs to people just like this. You must become like a child if you want to enter my kingdom." Then Jesus blessed each child.

# Blessed Are You

Jesus wanted his followers to know that trusting God will bring us happiness on earth and in heaven, too.

He told them, "Blessed are the people who are poor in spirit because they will live in the kingdom of heaven. Blessed are those that mourn. They will find comfort."

These words sounded strange to those who heard him. One disciple whispered to his friend, "How can a poor person be blessed? How does someone mourn and be blessed at the same time?"

Jesus went on, "Blessed are the meek for all the earth will be theirs. Blessed are those who are hungry for what is right and good. They will be satisfied. Blessed are the merciful for they will receive mercy. Blessed are the pure in heart. They will see God. Blessed are the people who make peace, because they are the children of God. You

are blessed even if you are persecuted for loving God and doing what is right because the kingdom of heaven will belong to you."

Jesus taught them that joy, blessing, and happiness can be found in loving God and loving others no matter what the circumstances.

Another day Jesus sat on a hill. Many people gathered to hear him preach. He said, "Treat others the way you would like to be treated."

A man wondered, "What about those who hurt you?"

"Pray for your enemies," Jesus said. "Remember that God loves even those who do wrong."

Later, one of his Apostles asked, "Jesus, how should we pray?"

Jesus told them, "Pray like this:

> 'Our Father, who art in heaven, hallowed be thy name. Thy kingdom come, thy will be done on earth as it is in heaven. Give us this day our daily bread. And forgive us our trespasses as we forgive those who trespass against us. Lead us not into temptation but deliver us from evil. Amen.'"

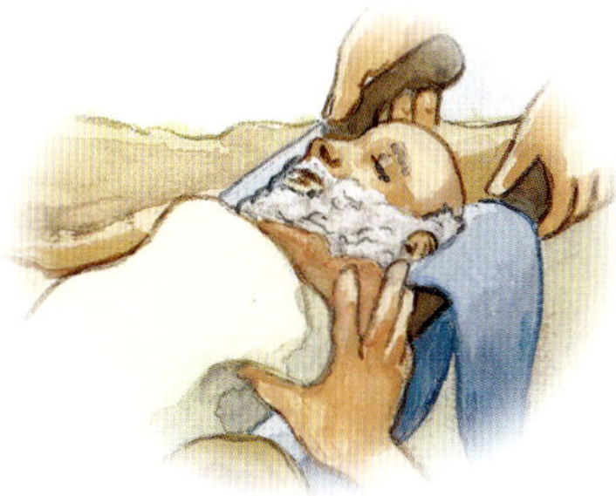

# Jesus Heals

"I'm sure Jesus can cure him," a man said to his three friends. The four men carried their paralyzed friend on a stretcher.

Jesus was in a house teaching. So many people had gathered that the house was full and a large group of people stood outside it.

The man asked the crowd, "Can you please make room for us to pass?"

But, no one moved. Everyone wanted to stay close to Jesus.

"I have an idea," he said to his friends. "Let's climb to the roof."

Before long, they made a hole in the roof. Then they carefully lowered their friend into the room.

Jesus noticed the deep faith of the paralyzed man's friends. He told the paralyzed man, "Your sins are forgiven."

"Only God can forgive sins!" someone in the crowd shouted.

Jesus said to the man lying on the cot, "Get up and walk. You are healed." At once the man stood up.

"Jesus healed him!" the crowd cried.

"Go home and sin no more," Jesus told the healed man.

Full of joy, the man and his friends left.

Jesus often showed the power of God's love by healing people of their physical illnesses and their sins.

One of the worst diseases of that time was leprosy. There was no cure for it, and people who suffered from this skin disease were forced to live apart from the community. They could only rejoin their families and friends if a priest said they were completely well.

Once, when Jesus and his Apostles were traveling to Jerusalem, they came upon ten people who had leprosy. The lepers called out, "Jesus, have mercy!"

Jesus stopped and looked at the lepers. "Go and show yourselves to the priests," he said.

On their way, every one of them was healed! One healed man returned to Jesus.

"Thank you, Jesus Master!" he said as he kneeled.

"Ten were healed. Where are the others?" Jesus asked. "Are you the only one who came back to give glory to God?"

"Yes, Lord, only me," the man replied.

"Get up and go," Jesus said. "Your faith is the reason you are healed."

# Crowds and Miracles

Jesus' teaching and healing made him so popular that crowds followed him wherever he went. One day there were 5,000 men—not counting all the women and children—listening to Jesus preach. Close to the end of the day, the Apostles became worried.

One of the Apostles spoke to Jesus. "You should send the people home. It's late, and they need to eat."

"Feed them yourselves," Jesus answered.

The Apostles did not know how they could feed so many people. They searched for anyone in the crowd who had food to share. They found only one person.

"All we could find was this boy," said an Apostle. "He has only five loaves of bread and two fish."

"That is more than enough," Jesus said with a smile.

"Have the people sit down in groups."

Then Jesus took the bread and the fish. He looked up to heaven and said a blessing over the food. He broke the bread and gave it back to the Apostles.

"Feed the people," he said.

The Apostles passed out the food and everyone ate. When everyone had finished and could not eat any more, there were twelve baskets of food left over!

Another evening, after teaching the crowds all day long, Jesus said to his friends, "Take the boat to the other side of the lake. I will stay and send the people home."

The Apostles got into Peter's boat and left. But in the middle of the night it got very windy. The little boat was tossed by the high waves. Then the Apostles saw something amazing. It looked like a man walking toward them on the water.

It was Jesus! He called out, "Do not be afraid!"

Peter replied, "Lord, let me come to you."

"Come," Jesus told him.

Peter got out of the boat and walked on the water toward Jesus. Before long Peter noticed the wind. He looked down at the swirling sea instead of at Jesus. Peter grew afraid and started to sink.

"Help me, Jesus!" he cried.

Jesus caught Peter's arm and pulled him up.

"Why did you doubt?" Jesus asked.

When they got into the boat the wind stopped. The Apostles then worshipped Jesus and said, "You are the Son of God!"

# Transfiguration

"Peter, James, and John," Jesus called. "I'd like to go up the mountain to pray. Will the three of you come with me?"

Jesus and the three disciples climbed until they reached the top. The Apostles waited quietly as Jesus prayed.

Suddenly, everything began to change. Jesus' clothes started to shine and looked as white as snow. Elijah the prophet and Moses appeared next to Jesus. They spoke with Jesus about what would soon happen to him. The three Apostles could hardly believe their eyes. Moses and Elijah had died centuries before!

"Lord," Peter called out. "It is good that we are here!"

Next a cloud overshadowed them. And they heard a voice say, "This is my Son, whom I love. Listen to him."

Peter, James, and John were frightened and they hid their faces. When it was quiet, they looked around. There was no one else there except Jesus. His clothes were no longer blindingly bright.

As they climbed down the mountain, Peter, James, and John couldn't stop thinking about what they had seen. Jesus said to them, "Don't tell anyone about this until I rise from the dead."

*Rise from the dead?* Peter wondered what Jesus meant.

# Hosanna!

It had been three years since Jesus began his mission at the wedding in Cana. He had traveled all over the country telling everyone he met how much God loves them.

The feast of Passover was approaching and Jesus and his friends—like all faithful Jews—went to Jerusalem.

When they were near the city, Jesus spoke to two of his disciples. “Go ahead of us. You will find a young donkey tied there. Untie it and bring it to me.”

The disciples looked worried. “Master, they might think we’re stealing it,” one said.

“If anyone asks you why you are taking the donkey,” Jesus said, “tell them ‘The Lord needs to use it.’”

It happened exactly as Jesus said it would. There was a donkey tied in front of a house. A man who saw them untie it asked what they were doing. The disciples answered as Jesus had told them and they were not bothered again.

When they returned with the donkey, Jesus rode it through the gates of Jerusalem. As he entered the city, people threw their cloaks on the ground before him. Others took leafy branches and waved them in the air or laid them on the path before Jesus.

The large crowd called out with joyful praise to God for all the powerful works Jesus had done. They shouted, "Hosanna! Blessed is he who comes in the name of the Lord!"

The people did this to give Jesus a royal welcome. But not everyone was happy with what Jesus had been teaching or doing.

Some of the religious leaders decided that Jesus was a problem. "It is time to get rid of this troublemaker once and for all," the high priest said. "We do not need someone

who claims to know God better than we do." So they paid one of the Apostles, Judas Iscariot, thirty pieces of silver to show them where to capture Jesus. From that moment, Judas Iscariot looked for an opportunity to betray Jesus.

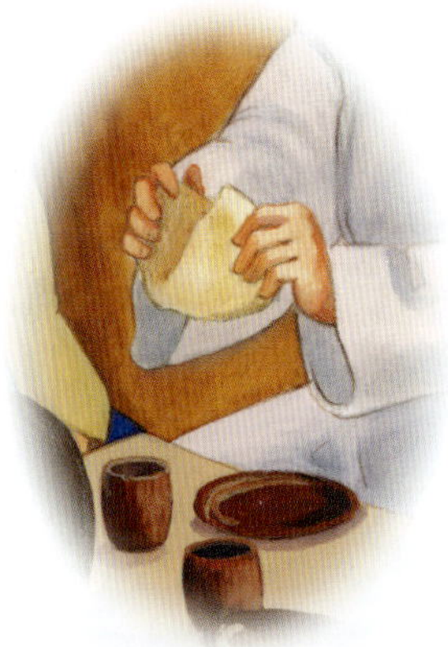

# The Last Supper

Jesus knew that Judas Iscariot would betray him. But Jesus wanted to do the Father's will. So he sent Peter and John to prepare a room for Passover.

When they returned, Peter said to Jesus, "All is as you said it would be. The room is ready, Master."

"Well done," Jesus responded. "Tonight we'll celebrate the Passover."

That evening, when they were together in the Upper Room, Jesus took off his outer robe. Then he took water and a basin and knelt on the floor in front of his Apostles.

"Come, I will wash your feet," he said.

Peter jumped up. "Never, my Lord! You will never wash my feet."

"If you do not allow me to serve you, then you cannot be a part of my mission," said Jesus.

Peter bowed his head. "Then wash my hands and face as well, Master."

Jesus washed the feet of all his Apostles. Then he told them, "I am your Master, but I have washed your feet. You must do the same to others. In order to be leaders, you must serve others."

Then, they all sat to share the meal. Jesus took the bread in his hands. He blessed it, broke it, and gave it to his friends. He said to them, "Take and eat. This is my Body which is given for you." Then he took the cup of wine. He blessed it and gave it to his disciples. Jesus said, "Take and drink. This is the cup of my Blood. It is the new covenant which is poured out for you."

While the other Apostles were enjoying the first Eucharist, Jesus saw someone leave. Judas Iscariot took one last look at Jesus before he walked out into the night.

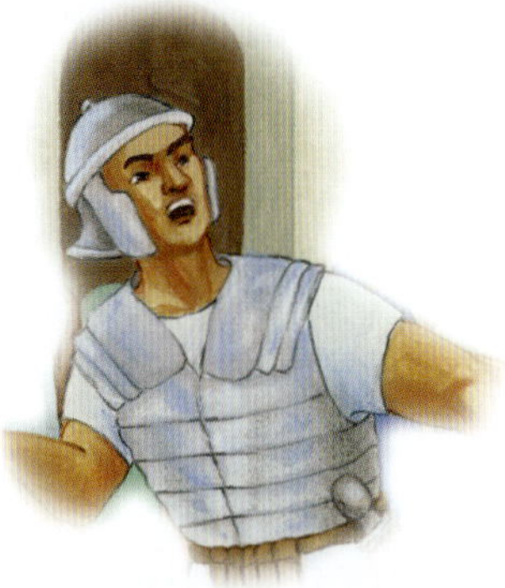

# Arrested

After they had finished the Passover meal, Jesus and the Apostles walked to Gethsemane—a nearby garden. He asked Peter, James, and John to pray with him.

Jesus went apart from them and prayed. "Father, I know that soon I will die. I don't want to suffer and die, but I want to do your will."

After a while, Jesus got up to talk to Peter. But Peter and the others had fallen asleep. Jesus woke them up and again asked them to pray with him. Then he prayed to God the Father once more. Meanwhile, Peter, James, and John fell sleep again.

Just after Jesus had woken up the disciples the second time, he heard the sound of marching. Soon they saw Judas Iscariot leading soldiers through the garden. Judas led them right to Jesus!

Judas had told the soldiers that the man he kissed on the cheek was the man they were looking for.

Jesus said to Judas Iscariot, “Do what you came to do.”

Judas kissed Jesus’ cheek and the soldiers arrested Jesus. Jesus’ friends ran off into the darkness. They were afraid they would be arrested, too.

Peter, however, followed close behind the soldiers. He stood by the fire outside the building where they had taken Jesus. A maid recognized Peter and said, “I know you. You’re a follower of Jesus!”

“I am not,” said Peter.

Later, another person standing around the fire said, “I saw you with Jesus.”

“No,” Peter denied again. “I said I don’t know him.”

A servant insisted, “I saw you in the garden with him.”

Peter walked quickly away from the fire, saying, “You’re wrong. I was not with him. I don’t even know who he is!”

Then Peter heard a rooster crow. He remembered that Jesus had once told him, “Before you hear the rooster crow, you will deny me three times.” Peter hung his head in shame and cried. He had betrayed his friend and Savior.

# Condemned to Death

The soldiers brought Jesus to the governor, Pontius Pilate. He asked Jesus, "Is it true that you're a king?"

Jesus answered quietly, "If I had an earthly kingdom, my subjects would be here to defend me. My kingdom is not here."

Pontius Pilate was confused. *He doesn't seem like a criminal*, Pilate thought. *But the Jewish leaders insist that Jesus is a rebel. If I release Jesus, will the Jews cause a riot?*

"Take him away to be whipped," Pilate ordered.

The soldiers beat him cruelly. Then they wove thorny branches into a circle. One soldier pressed it down onto Jesus' head.

"It's your very own crown!" the soldier mocked. "Now you look like a king!" The others laughed at seeing Jesus in so much pain.

When the soldiers brought Jesus back to the palace, he and another man named Barabbas were brought to stand in front of a crowd.

Pilate spoke to the crowd. “It is a tradition that I free one prisoner during your feast of Passover. Shall I free Barabbas or Jesus?”

The people who didn’t like Jesus yelled, “Barabbas!” Louder and louder they yelled. “Free Barabbas!”

“And what about Jesus?” Pilate asked.

“Crucify him!” they shouted in return.

Pilate did not believe that Jesus was guilty of any crime. But he was afraid of the crowd and so Pilate washed his hands and said, “Take Jesus and crucify him!”

# Carrying the Cross

Because of Pilate's command, the soldiers laid a wooden Cross on Jesus' shoulder and bloody back.

Jesus had to carry the heavy Cross all the way to the hill outside the city. He was so weak from the beatings he had suffered that he fell. Wanting to do the Father's will, Jesus got up and continued.

Shortly after his fall, he came face to face with his mother. Mary reached out to him as tears flowed down her face. Blood trickled down Jesus' face as he gazed at her.

"My son," Mary said.

"Mother," whispered Jesus. Then a soldier pushed him and the painful ordeal continued.

Noticing that Jesus walked slowly, another soldier grabbed a man who was passing by and shouted, "Get over there and help him carry the Cross!"

Simon of Cyrene took his place beside Jesus and the two continued on the narrow street toward Calvary.

Many people followed Jesus as the group of soldiers whipped and prodded him forward. Despite Simon's help with the Cross, Jesus crashed to the ground again.

Jesus was in agony. He hurt all over his body. Then he heard the wails of some women who were following. He looked at them with love and compassion. "Women of Jerusalem, don't cry for me," he managed to say. "Cry for your own suffering and the suffering of your children."

Jesus continued step by step until he reached Calvary where criminals were executed by crucifixion.

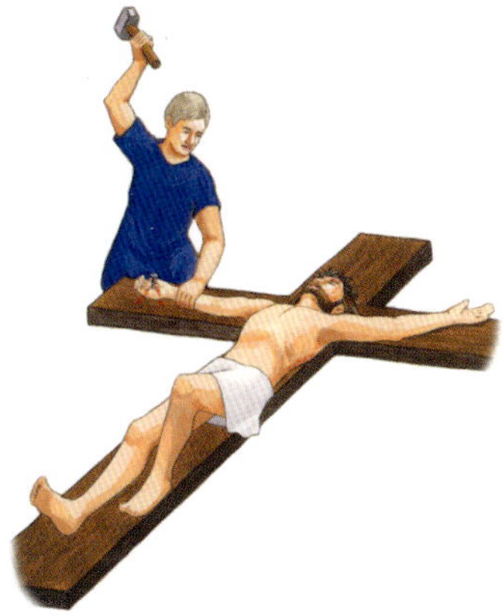

# Death on a Cross

Mary watched as the soldiers stripped Jesus of his clothing and laid him on the wooden beam. The only Apostle who was present was John. He did his best to comfort Jesus' mother while the soldiers nailed Jesus' hands and feet to the Cross.

Two criminals were crucified that same day. One of them made fun of Jesus. "Why don't you save yourself and us?" he mocked.

The other crucified man replied, "We deserve punishment because we have done wrong. Jesus is innocent!" Then he turned to Jesus and said, "Lord, remember me when you come to your kingdom."

"Today, you will share in the kingdom of God," Jesus promised him.

As Jesus grew weaker, Mary and the Apostle John remained at the foot of his Cross. The other Apostles were too frightened to be there. With Mary and John was a woman named Mary Magdalene. She was a loyal follower of Jesus.

Jesus looked down at his mother. “This is your son,” Jesus said as he indicated John. Then he looked at John and said, “This is your mother.” From then on, John took care of Mary as if she were his own mother. Jesus was grateful that his mother would not be alone.

Jesus then prayed. “Father, I put my life in your hands.” With that he bowed his head, took his last rasping breath, and died. At that moment the earth shook and the sky became dark.

A disciple of Jesus named Joseph, from the town of Arimathea, was there. He asked Pontius Pilate for permission to bury Jesus’ body. Another of Jesus’ followers, Nicodemus, brought the spices traditionally used for burial. They carefully took Jesus down from the Cross. They wrapped his body in linen and placed it in a new tomb in a garden.

Mary Magdalene and some other women who had also followed Jesus paid attention to where Jesus was buried. As it was almost the Sabbath, the women would have to return on the day after the holy day to finish the burial rituals. Mary Magdalene watched as Joseph and some other men sealed Jesus’ tomb with a huge stone.

# Alive!

Early in the morning after the Sabbath—on the first day of the week—Mary Magdalene and some other women went to Jesus' tomb. They went to finish some of the rituals that were done when a person's body was buried. Although it was still dark, Mary Magdalene could see that the stone had been removed. Looking inside the tomb, she discovered that Jesus' body wasn't there!

She ran to tell Peter and the others the news. The Apostles Peter and John hurried to the tomb.

"Mary Magdalene was right," said Peter. "Jesus' body is not here!"

After returning to the tomb, Mary Magdalene began to cry. *Who could have taken his body?* she wondered. Then Mary Magdalene heard a sound. *It must be the gardener*, she thought.

"Did you take Jesus away?" she asked. "Please tell me where you have put his body."

The man smiled at her and said, "Mary!"

Mary Magdalene jumped to her feet. She recognized the voice. *It's Jesus!* she realized. "Rabboni . . . teacher!" she happily called out.

"Go and tell my friends that I am going to my Father and their Father," Jesus said.

Mary went as fast as she could to spread the wonderful news. Jesus was alive!

# A Mysterious Companion

"I really believed he was the Messiah," one man said to his friend. The two were walking to the town of Emmaus. They were followers of Jesus.

As the two disciples continued to discuss Jesus' suffering, crucifixion, and death, a man they did not recognize joined them.

"What are you talking about?" he asked.

"Don't you know what happened in Jerusalem?" the disciples replied.

"What happened?" the man asked.

"Jesus was killed," one of the disciples said. "We believed he was the Messiah—the Savior God promised to send."

The other disciple added, "We thought he would save Israel. But he was crucified, so we must have been wrong."

“You don’t understand what is written in Scripture,” the man said. He told them that the Savior needed to suffer and die to save all people.

The two disciples felt their hearts beating fast as they listened to the man explain God’s word to them.

When night fell, the disciples invited the man to supper. The three men sat down and the food was served. The two disciples watched as the man took the bread, blessed it, and broke it for them to eat. Immediately, the disciples realized that their mysterious companion was Jesus!

As soon as they recognized Jesus, he disappeared. They were filled with joy because they had seen the risen Lord!

“Let’s return to Jerusalem at once,” said one of the disciples. “We have to let Peter and the others know that Jesus is alive!”

# Jesus Returns to the Father

Despite Jesus' resurrection, the Apostles were still frightened that they too could be arrested like Jesus had been. They preferred to pray, eat, and sleep behind locked doors. One evening Jesus appeared in the room with them, but they did not recognize him.

"Don't be afraid," Jesus said. "It is I!"

His friends looked at Jesus in astonishment. He asked, "May I have something to eat, too?"

Someone offered Jesus a plate of fish, and he ate it.

"Ghosts don't eat," said one of the Apostles. "It's really our Lord, Jesus!"

Jesus remained forty days with his disciples. He ate with them, walked with them, taught them, and answered their questions. His Apostles and friends were so happy. They knew what Mary, his mother, had known all along: Jesus was God's Son.

One morning, Jesus appeared to some of the Apostles who had been fishing. Jesus asked Peter, "Do you love me?" Jesus asked the question three times and three times Peter said that he loved Jesus.

"Then take care of my sheep," Jesus replied each time.

Peter had denied Jesus three times on the night of Jesus' arrest. Now, Jesus gave Peter the chance to proclaim his love three times. Peter was grateful for Jesus' forgiveness.

On the fortieth day after Jesus' resurrection from the dead, he and his disciples walked up a large hill.

Jesus blessed his friends and reminded them that he promised to be with them forever. He asked them to continue his mission.

"Teach everyone about God's kingdom . . . even to the ends of the earth," he said. "The Holy Spirit will come to you and help you."

With that Jesus began to ascend to heaven. He said, "I am going back to the Father. Return to the city, and wait for the Holy Spirit."

As the disciples gazed into the sky, two men in white robes suddenly appeared.

"Why are you looking toward heaven?" one of them asked. "Jesus has been taken from you, but one day he will return in the same way."

# The Church Is Born

After Jesus' ascension to heaven, his disciples went to the Upper Room in Jerusalem where some of them had stayed since the Last Supper. Mary, Jesus' mother, was with them. Together they prayed, sang, and waited for the Holy Spirit.

The Jewish feast of Pentecost fell on the tenth day after Jesus ascended into heaven. People from many different countries who spoke many different languages were in Jerusalem for this religious celebration.

That day Mary and Jesus' Apostles were gathered together praying. Suddenly a great roar of wind filled the tiny room! Flames of fire appeared and rested on each one of them. They were immediately filled with the gifts of the Holy Spirit to help them spread the Good News of Jesus around the world.

The now courageous Apostles left the Upper Room and spoke about Jesus to everyone. Peter told the crowd that Jesus, who had been crucified and rose from the dead, was the Lord and the promised Messiah.

"Be sorry for your sins and be baptized!" he said. "You will receive the Holy Spirit!"

The people who were there heard and understood what the Apostles preached even though they all spoke different languages. Many people came to believe that Jesus is the Messiah. About 3,000 people were baptized on that day. It was the beginning of the Church.

# Conclusion

Jesus is the second person of the Holy Trinity and the Savior of the world. He came so that all our sins could be forgiven and so that we can someday go to live with God in heaven. Knowing about the life, death, resurrection, and ascension of Jesus can help us grow close to him.

Prayer helps us to grow close to Jesus, too. We can spend time with Jesus every day in prayer, just like we would spend time with a friend. We can talk to Jesus anytime—whether we are sad or happy, afraid or confident, alone or with others.

We can also strengthen our relationship with Jesus by receiving the sacraments. Jesus is present in the Eucharist in a special way. He gave us this gift at the Last Supper. At each Mass, the priest repeats Jesus' words, "This is my Body" and "This is my Blood." The bread and wine actually become the Body and Blood of Jesus although it looks and tastes like bread and wine. We share in the life of Jesus when we share Holy Communion. We can adore the real presence of Jesus in the Eucharist. We kneel or genuflect before the tabernacle because Jesus—our Lord and Savior—is truly present there!

Every time we treat other people like Jesus wants us to, we grow closer to him. When we sin and we are sorry, Jesus is waiting to give us his mercy. Jesus is the Word God speaks and the love in our hearts.

Have you talked with Jesus today?

# Who are the Daughters of St. Paul?

We are Catholic sisters with a mission. Our task is to bring the love of Jesus to everyone like Saint Paul did. You can find us in over 50 countries. Our founder, Blessed James Alberione, showed us how to reach out to the world through the media. That's why we publish books, make movies and apps, record music, broadcast on radio, perform concerts, help people at our bookstores, visit parishes, host JClub book fairs, use social media and the Internet, and pray for all of you.

Pauline
BOOKS & MEDIA

The Daughters of St. Paul operate book and media centers at the following addresses. Visit, call, or write the one nearest you today, or find us at www.paulinestore.org.

**CALIFORNIA**
3908 Sepulveda Blvd, Culver City, CA 90230 — 310-397-8676
3250 Middlefield Road, Menlo Park, CA 94025 — 650-369-4230

**FLORIDA**
145 SW 107th Avenue, Miami, FL 33174 — 305-559-6715

**HAWAII**
1143 Bishop Street, Honolulu, HI 96813 — 808-521-2731

**ILLINOIS**
172 North Michigan Avenue, Chicago, IL 60601 — 312-346-4228

**LOUISIANA**
4403 Veterans Memorial Blvd, Metairie, LA 70006 — 504-887-7631

**MASSACHUSETTS**
885 Providence Hwy, Dedham, MA 02026 — 781-326-5385

**MISSOURI**
9804 Watson Road, St. Louis, MO 63126 — 314-965-3512

**NEW YORK**
115 E. 29th Street, New York City, NY 10016 — 212-754-1110

**SOUTH CAROLINA**
243 King Street, Charleston, SC 29401 — 843-577-0175

**TEXAS**
No book center; for parish exhibits or outreach evangelization, contact: 210-569-0500 or SanAntonio@paulinemedia.com or P.O. Box 761416, San Antonio, TX 78245

**VIRGINIA**
1025 King Street, Alexandria, VA 22314 — 703-549-3806

**CANADA**
3022 Dufferin Street, Toronto, ON M6B 3T5 — 416-781-9131

**SMILE** God loves you!